Silhouettes

Silhouettes

Contemporary Paper Cutting Projects

Sharyn Sowell

LARK BOOKS
A Division of Sterling Publishing Co., Inc.
New York / London

Senior Editor
Terry Taylor

Editor
Larry Shea

Assistant Editor
Mark Bloom

Art Director
Kathleen Holmes

Photographer:
Stewart O'Shields

Cover Designer
Chris Bryant

Library of Congress Cataloging-in-Publication Data

Sowell, Sharyn.
   Silhouettes : contemporary paper cutting projects / Sharyn Sowell.—1st ed.
      p.   cm.
   Includes index.
   ISBN 978-1-60059-278-2 (pb-trade pbk. : alk. paper)
   1. Paper work.   2. Silhouettes.   I. Title.
TT870.S6725 2009
736'.984—dc22

                          2008032656

10 9 8 7 6 5 4 3 2 1

First Edition

Published by Lark Books, A Division of Sterling Publishing Co., Inc.
387 Park Avenue South, New York, NY 10016

Text and illustrations © 2009, Sharyn Sowell
Photography © 2009, Lark Books unless otherwise specified

Distributed in Canada by Sterling Publishing, c/o Canadian Manda Group,
165 Dufferin Street
Toronto, Ontario, Canada M6K 3H6

Distributed in the United Kingdom by GMC Distribution Services,
Castle Place, 166 High Street, Lewes, East Sussex, England BN7 1XU

Distributed in Australia by Capricorn Link (Australia) Pty Ltd.,
P.O. Box 704, Windsor, NSW 2756 Australia

If you have questions or comments about this book, please contact:
Lark Books
67 Broadway
Asheville, NC 28801
828-253-0467

Manufactured in China

ISBN 13: 978-1-60059-278-2

For information about custom editions, special sales, premium and corporate purchases, please contact Sterling Special Sales Department at 800-805-5489 or specialsales@sterlingpub.com.

Contents

Introduction

Do you remember cutting your first silhouette? I cut my first using Swiss army knife scissors and an empty lunch bag while sitting in a rowboat. No kidding!

Now, thousands of images later, I am more smitten than ever with the art and craft of the silhouette. Using scissors, a knife, or a brush, you can create beautifully expressive silhouettes that are reminiscent of the past, yet fresh as tomorrow.

Take a look at my creative process throughout this book. I give you the tricks you'd learn peeking over my shoulder at work. Because you never have enough hours in the day, I've included projects that are quick and easy. You'll fashion ready-made pillows into custom works of art in just an hour or two (page 30). You'll work magic with ordinary foam board, turning it into a stunning focal point (page 90). Take a clock from ho-hum to incredible with a few snips to a sheet of paper (page 36).

These projects won't break the bank, either. The materials are minimal and inexpensive. You could even pick up items in a thrift store if you're on a tight budget. You'll see how you can create chic accents for your home, whether your style is clean and contemporary, feminine and cozy, or country rustic.

I'll show you how to use your digital camera to transform a basic wall into one your friends won't stop talking about (page 58). We'll transform a simple framed photo into a family heirloom by adding a hand-cut paper silhouette (page 97). If you're planning a dinner party, use the patterns to cut paper into elegant votive holders, napkin rings, and coasters (pages 33 and 51). Sophistication doesn't have to take hours, but let's keep that our secret, shall we?

You don't have to be a creative genius. I've included easy instructions, broken down into a few simple steps. Nothing's terribly complicated. In the back of the book, I've provided the actual patterns for the projects—and, as a bonus, lots of fun variations—to jump-start your creativity. If you're the incurably independent type, you might prefer to cut your own silhouettes freehand as I do. I'll show you how to do that too.

Because I'm me and you're you, my silhouettes have a unique look. Yours will reflect you the same way. But now it's my turn to share. Turn the page and peek over my shoulder—together, we'll discover a wonderful world of silhouette projects to transform your home.

The Basics

There are no rules for silhouettes. Isn't that a relief? You get to make your own rules as you go, exploring what works and what doesn't. Today, making silhouettes is an art for those of us who love this historical craft but want to give it a modern look. And you can achieve that look in a myriad of ways.

Silhouettes can be boldly modern, sweetly feminine, classically elegant, or downright quirky. Put any spin on them you wish; silhouettes will flex with you to fit whatever creative dreams you have.

When you're learning any new craft, knowing a few basics will help you avoid some common but troublesome pitfalls. Let's go over a few bare-bones essentials to get you started.

Basic Tools

You can incorporate silhouettes into almost any crafting project. Stencil a silhouette of your one-year-old baby onto birthday cupcakes, etch a glass pitcher with your family crest (even if you just made it up), or cut a silhouette to iron onto a pillowcase. Whatever craft medium you enjoy, you can use tools and materials you already have to bring silhouette designs into your projects.

You don't need a vast arsenal of specialized tools to master the art of making a silhouette. If you're like most crafty types, you probably already have just about everything you need to begin. Some tools, however, you'll find handy regardless of the specific medium and project you choose.

Pencils are an absolute necessity. Any type will do as long as it's sharp enough to give you a crisp, clear line when you sketch or transfer a pattern. Because pencils are so cheap, I indulge in whatever ones strike my fancy—nifty mechanical pencils, traditional wooden ones, carpenter's pencils, white and colored ones, even watercolor pencils. Keeping a variety on hand will enable you to experiment wildly, leading to all sorts of unforeseen fun.

Erasers always come in handy since no one is perfect. My favorites are white plastic erasers, but you may prefer kneadable erasers or the standard pink rubber kind. Erasers now come in long, thin pencil or pen styles as well as the more familiar rectangles.

Transfer paper or carbon paper is helpful if you plan to trace patterns.

Scissors are the most-often-used tool for creating a silhouette. It's a treat to have a nice selection, but you can make do with just a basic pair or two. Paper dulls scissors over time, so don't ask your best fabric scissors to do double duty. Start with whatever you've got on hand. When it's time for a splurge, shop for a pair with fine tips, which can be invaluable when you're working on tiny details. Basic office scissors, embroidery or nail scissors, sewing scissors, and craft shears are all good, solid tools. To create unusual outlines, I enjoy using fancy shaped craft scissors and pinking shears as well.

A craft knife and spare blades are essential for slicing through materials too thick or hard for scissors. A standard lightweight craft knife will satisfy most needs, but buy a heavyweight knife for bigger projects. Using a little tool for a big job isn't safe. Be sure to store your knives in a box or covered by the small shields they came with.

Self-healing cutting mats must be part of your tool stash if you plan to use a craft knife. Never cut on a hard surface because it can damage the blade, ruin the surface, and even injure you. If you don't have a rubber mat, use a thick piece of cardboard as a temporary cutting board.

Rulers and t-squares are fundamental to your success as a crafter. You'll need them to size designs to fit your materials, line images up straight, and decide where to cut. I am smitten with transparent triangular architect's rulers that allow you to see the material below. The metal ones with a thin cork backing stay in place well, and there's nothing sweeter for bigger projects than a deliciously long yardstick. T-squares make right angles a snap. You don't need a selection of rulers—just one will do—but they're so cheap, you may as well become a connoisseur. I am!

An iron and ironing board can rescue you when paper and fabric become uneven or limp. Both materials warp when cut and wrinkle at all the wrong moments. Use a dry, not-too-hot iron with an ironing board to press them flat. When working with delicate fabric, have a pressing cloth at hand. Never use steam; it can cause water damage.

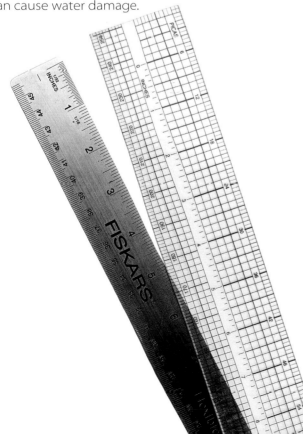

A Place for Your Stuff

Whether you're crafting in a roomy studio or a tiny corner, you'll need a place to store your tools, supplies, and unfinished projects. Large plastic bins that slide under the bed or sofa can be a practical solution. Flat drawers in cupboards specially made for art materials are good for storing sheets of paper. You can also use a small filing box for standard-size sheets of paper and roll larger pieces into cardboard tubes, available at floor covering stores (from rolls of carpet) and at office supply stores. Stacking plastic boxes, crates, and even the humble shoebox will suffice for small items like glue sticks, vials of glitter, and knives and scissors. When I began, I used a rusty fishing tackle box and a sturdy cardboard box left over from my son's science project to hide all my supplies in the back of a closet. Now I tuck many of my supplies into vintage suitcases and covered cake tins, and even an old dollhouse. Use whatever fits your decorating style and your budget.

Basic Supplies

Because you can incorporate silhouettes into almost any art form, most of the projects in this book will easily adapt to whatever craft is your passion. You may already have a stash of crafting supplies for your favorite medium. Hang onto them; you'll still need them. There are, however, some basic materials we'll use, regardless of the specific craft.

First, the obvious: paper. You can use papers of all sizes and colors to create silhouettes. Black is the traditional favorite, but modern silhouette artists like to experiment with unexpected twists of color and texture. With so many deliciously seductive papers available at a reasonable price, you'll probably move beyond basic black sooner than later.

Collecting paper over a long period of time gives you lots of choices when you're in the middle of a project and don't want to stop. I've got a stash to rival a small store, and it's almost like shopping in my favorite boutique when I open my studio door. You can do the same on your own scale by buying a few pieces at a time; even the most limited budget can afford a few juicy sheets every week.

Text-weight, general-purpose papers are readily available, usually in standard 8½ x 11-inch (21.6 x 27.9 cm) sheets. Most are acid free, a fact you can usually confirm with just a glance at the label. Forest-certified, recycled, and non-tree fiber papers are all commonly available and clearly labeled as such. Buy in bulk packages or single sheets from office supply, scrapbook, craft, printing supply, or copy shops. Choose mostly solid colors; they are far more versatile than patterned papers. I store a rainbow of choices in see-through plastic boxes, which helps me find just the right one when I need it.

Card stock is heavier than text-weight paper and is often found in 8½ x 11-inch (21.6 x 27.9 cm) or 12 x 12-inch (30.5 x 30.5 cm) sheets. These colorful papers are often sold for scrapbooking. Larger sheets are available in flat bins in the craft supply aisle as well. Card stock is harder to cut than text-weight paper, but you should still be able to manage simple shapes. You'll love these papers for backgrounds as well. Pick up a variety to give yourself a choice while working.

Gift wrap paper in roll or sheet form can often be a pretty and practical alternative. Choose finer quality papers. Flimsy, lightweight paper won't produce beautiful results; this is a case where cheap is not a bargain. Use this versatile paper for all jobs, from small silhouettes to dramatic cut-paper curtains. Attractive solid colors and tiny prints are more useful than larger prints.

Butcher paper and bulletin board paper, those tried-and-true cheapskate's friends, are available in any well-stocked teaching or arts and crafts store, sold by the yard at a price that will leave you grinning. Often not acid free, this paper still has a million uses: I cut curtains from it, wrap and decorate gifts with simple silhouettes, and draw patterns across its large, inexpensive span. I always have some around because I can cut giant swaths with nary a thought about the cost.

Watercolor, printmaking, and other heavy fine art papers can be hard to slice through, so choose the lightest weight available. These papers are appealing because you can alter the papers' appearance any way you choose. Consider incorporating watercolors, rubber stamps, airbrush, and acrylics into your latest project. Embellish before you cut.

Tissue paper, magazines and newspapers, even phone books can provide free paper to use for practice. I never throw away a phone book. Scissors at the ready, I slice my way through sheet after sheet. Seldom do I save this work, but it's a great way to experiment. When you want to practice, pull out a phone book and cut away while waiting at the soccer field or listening to the music while on hold.

Old books, sheet music, and other vintage papers are fair game for cutting. Scan old papers to print out on acid free paper or use color copies to save the originals. Old paper cut or used as background can add just the right touch to certain silhouettes, especially if you're aiming for a heritage flavor.

Wallpaper is frequently available for almost nothing on clearance and has a myriad of uses: cut up into murals and placemats, glued down as silhouettes on a floor, even woven or stuck together in layers to make rug-like floor mats. You can find wallpaper made of vinyl, paper, even linen, bamboo, and other exotic materials, so gear your choice to the project you've got in mind.

Tracing paper, though not a necessity, can make altering designs a snap. I use layers of tracing paper to check the fit of a design on a product, penciling in hints of the shape and laying it over something I want to craft. This way I can see if the silhouette needs to be enlarged or reduced. You can also use it for copying patterns. Tracing paper has a million uses.

Decorative art papers come in a wide array—from marbled and gilded sheets to rice, grass, bamboo, silk, and even banana leaf papers. Choose acid free papers, and if you're planning a cutout, avoid heavily fibrous pieces because they don't cut easily or evenly. Their ragged edges distort the clean lines of a silhouette and are prone to fraying. While thick-strand papers are difficult to cut, they make backgrounds that are as practical as they are sumptuous.

Glues and adhesives must be part of your supply stash. Keep a nice assortment on hand. Specific choices depend on what materials you use. But the bottles and glue sticks you've already got in your craft cupboard are probably good enough to get started. Branch out and sample new varieties when you shop. These products are so affordable, even a cheapskate like me can pick them up without thinking twice! Common white glue is a must, but acid-free pastes, iron-on fabric bonding materials, glue sticks, hot glue guns, dimensional dots, and double-stick tape are just a few of the wide array of options. Stay away from rubber cement and other acid-laden adhesives; they can deteriorate and ruin your beautiful work with alarming speed.

Assorted bits and oddments such as glitter, ribbon, inks, felt, contact paper, paints, and paintbrushes will enable you to add your own touch to the silhouette projects in this book, and whatever you have in your collection will no doubt prove wonderfully inspirational as you experiment with silhouettes.

No Construction Zone

In your search for new and exciting stenciling materials, you may be tempted to dip into your children's art supplies. In most cases that's a fine idea (and get the kids to work on the project with you!), but there is one material you should avoid. That pack of multi-colored construction paper looks great, but it is completely unsuitable for silhouettes. The fibrous nature and heavy acid content, coupled with very unstable colors, make construction paper a very poor choice for pieces intended to last. Use it only for practice or for projects that you don't intend to save and display past the weekend you made them.

Getting Started

Just as you won't need a raft of exotic supplies, you'll be glad to know you don't have to master a long list of grand techniques. The best way to learn silhouette art is to grab a pair of scissors and cut something—anything—out. Look at your design critically. What's pleasing about it? What needs improvement?
Try the same design over and over, and you'll see improvement.

What's great about paper silhouettes is slicing through paper with abandon and then saving only what tickles your eyes. You can toss the rest into the garbage and still feel elated with your work.

You can sketch first or not. Just get familiar with the way the shapes are formed. Remember that this is about the joy and adventure of the experience, not about perfect results. Ignore the perfectionist within

and enjoy the fun of creating. Refuse to be critical. This is your time to sit back and savor the freedom of a craft that doesn't require perfection.

Practice will teach you not to be too literal. You'll get a feel for your own personal style. Resist the temptation to copy someone else. Strike out on your own with confidence. Once you master the bare-bones basic techniques in this section, you'll see silhouettes everywhere you look. You'll ache to get your latest inspiration down on paper.

Since silhouettes are essentially an exercise in positive and negative space, understanding this concept is essential. Grab a pair of scissors and an ordinary piece of paper. Let's do a bit of paper play. Starting at an edge, cut half a circle. Lay the original piece of paper on the left side of your table, and then cut out the portion immediately to its right. The hole left by the paper you removed is negative space, and the piece you've cut is positive space.

Now let's get fancy. Pick up the cut-out piece again and cut another shape from it. Lay that cut out part into the negative space. After you've had a chance to look at it, pick it up and cut again and again, until you're tired of the game.

Design Basics

Silhouettes are works of art stripped down to the bare bones … no subtle gradients of color, no soft edges, no smudging, and no slight variations of tone or hue or value. As we learned earlier, silhouettes offer one stunning visual opportunity: positive and negative space.

Your stock in trade for this art form is hard edges and well-defined lines. It's a clean, clear, yes-or-no, black-or-white choice, at once demanding and freeing. You've got positive and negative space, that's it. You can use paint or paper, etching or fabric, embossing or stencils—any material or technique you can think of—but silhouettes, boiled down to the very essence, are simply positive and negative spaces playing off one another.

With a silhouette, it's easy to switch just one element of a design and achieve a sure-fire success by following just a few simple rules. When you want a big visual punch, for example, stick to designs that are slim on details and strong on contrast. Bold images and high-contrast colors drive home a look that really pops and carries a strong message. Images stripped down to the bare essentials give a bold, clean look that says "contemporary." Straight, geometric lines and simple shapes lend strength to the modern, streamlined look.

Color choices run the gamut. You can even stick to a single color as long as the contrast in texture is strong. For example, you might paint a wall in a matte texture, and then apply a silhouette in the same color except

with a sleek, glossy finish. You can make a pillow in a nubby chocolate brown wool and apply an ironed-on appliqué in a smooth silk that's the same warm chocolate color. Let the difference in texture show the silhouette.

Clear brights and sharply contrasting colors carry the bold look through a room, while muted or pale colors send a message that's more subtle and classic. Neutrals can flex to go contemporary or classic, primitive, country, or ethnic.

If you're aiming for a soft and soothing look, use detail and small scale. Quiet, gentle décor calls for subtle colors and similar values. Choose shades of green and coral, or select earthy tones that soothe rather than scream. Florals, botanicals, animals, and other natural themes reflect the calm of the outdoors. Choose organic shapes that bend and curve, avoiding straight lines. Repeat the pattern and cluster related images for the best effect.

Your First Silhouette

Some beginners prefer to follow a pattern closely, gathering experience one success at a time, while others strike out on their own from the start, sketching or creating silhouettes freehand. If you're new to the world of silhouettes, you probably fall into one of these two camps: results-oriented or exploration-oriented. If you're in the results-oriented camp, you may find patterns helpful. You'll gain experience by completing wonderful projects while avoiding disheartening failures. If you are in the exploration-oriented camp, dive right in and start cutting. It doesn't matter what you make or how it turns out. The lessons you learn along the way will ultimately serve you. Either path will develop your skills.

But where do you start?

First, decide how you want to use your silhouette. Do you want to make a big bold statement on the wall or merely add a decorative touch to a simple project like a scrapbook page? Measure your materials and decide what size you'd like the design to be. Adjust the size of the silhouette to fit. If you decided to work with a pattern, use a scanner and printer or a copy machine to adjust the pattern to the right size, and then print it out.

Double-check to make sure you're happy with the fit of the silhouette on your object (whatever it is), and then use transfer paper and pencil to copy the pattern onto the back of the object whenever

possible—obviously, you won't pencil-mark the back of a wall. Drawing on the back means nobody will ever see your pattern marks. We'll cover the basics of transferring patterns a little later in the section "Use a Pattern as a Basis" on page 26.

If you're in a pinch and want to copy a pattern onto paper, glass, or fabric, but you don't have transfer paper, here's a trick to solve the problem. Tape the paper with your pattern onto a window, with the printed side toward the glass. Now use a regular pencil to scribble along the edges of the pattern. Remove the paper from the glass and lay it on top of the object to cut. Use a pencil to draw along the lines. Now you're ready to go.

Remember that your finished product will always be the reverse of what you see when you look at your pattern marks, since you'll be turning the object over and viewing it from the "right" side when you're finished.

Feel free to use the patterns in this book to make as many of these items as you like for family, friends, and your own home use. But if you plan to sell your work, you must create your own images; the patterns provided are for personal use only.

Mounting Your Silhouette

Many of the projects in this book don't involve paper or glue, but because it's the most common way to make a silhouette, let's discuss how to stick paper down smoothly. It can be frustrating if you don't know how to do it properly, so let me share a few hard-won secrets that will help you avoid difficulty.

- If you're new to silhouettes, start by cutting simple shapes, which are easier to cut and attach. When you cut complex silhouettes in large sizes, the paper or fabric tends to warp. Even small variations in the backing surface or silhouette can form wrinkles or difficult irregularities that can ruin all your hard work.

- Before applying any adhesive, it's wise to lay the silhouette atop the backing material and check to make sure everything's perfect. If you lay everything out and notice the silhouette has warped slightly—or has any wrinkles, bends, or other imperfections—turn it upside down on your ironing board and give your paper a quick swipe with a warm, dry iron. Never use steam with paper or fabric!

- Use scraps to be certain the adhesive and the art materials are compatible before you glue the artwork. This simple step can save your project and prevent heartache.

Becoming Unglued

If you're mounting a silhouette and you notice an imperfection after the glue dries, don't try to pry it up to reposition it, as this seldom succeeds. If you've used water-soluble glue, here's a technique that might save your project. Don't try this unless your piece is fairly immune to water damage and you're desperate for a fix, because it may end up ruining the whole thing. But this little trick just might rescue a piece that would otherwise end up in the trash.

1. Spray a piece of fabric lightly with plain warm water so it's barely damp, not soaking.

2. Gently press the cloth against the back of the backing paper and leave it there for five minutes or so. Thick or water-resistant papers may take longer, and thin, porous papers and adhesives less time.

3. Turn the paper right side up and very carefully slip a knife or fingernail under the silhouette. Attempt to coax it away from the background paper. If it sticks, turn it back over and soak it a bit longer. You can try the steam from an iron held away half an inch (1.3 cm) or so from the silhouette.

If you're successful at removing the silhouette, let it dry, then iron it smooth and flat with a dry iron. You will need a new background.

- When possible, it's best to bond the entire surface at one time with the materials lying flat on a smooth surface. Smooth the material down to see if you need to make any adjustments, which you'll want to do before the adhesive sets. If your silhouette is large or complex, you may need to glue it in several sections. Work quickly and accurately so you can shift things a little if you need to adjust the fit. If you work too slowly or the glue sets too rapidly, you can end up with a bubble or wrinkle.

- Don't rub the silhouettes as you adhere them, as you can easily damage delicate papers or scratch the finish on a piece of glass. I often use the fleshy area of my arm between my wrist and elbow in a rolling motion, rather like a soft, human rolling pin. This technique is especially helpful when working with large pieces, when you have to stick down one area and then move to the next.

- Trying to mount a very large area at one time can be impossibly frustrating; it's much easier to work in segments that you can manage easily. The size you can handle depends mostly on the complexity of the silhouette. Old long-sleeved cotton shirts tossed over your usual clothing work wonderfully while you're gluing. They help you avoid arms covered in glue, and you can change shirts several times if necessary to stay neat during major projects.

- One last bit of advice: When it's time to make the bond, do it quickly while the adhesive is still pliable. I always hold my breath a bit because this is the most critical step. When finished, step back, admire your handiwork and breathe a sigh of relief. Whew!

Four Ways to Make a Silhouette

Now that we've covered the basic materials and tools, you may be saying, "Enough already! Let's cut to the chase and *make* something!" OK, ready to roll up your shirtsleeves and make silhouettes galore? There are no hard-and-fast rules, but you'll find it helpful to know the four basic ways of making a silhouette. Once you know these techniques, you can play with them as you would a versatile recipe, combining and interchanging the methods to suit yourself.

Cast a Shadow

Perhaps the oldest way to generate a silhouette image is the cast shadow method. Remember playing with your shadow on the playground? Making shadow puppets with your hands on a wall? Shadows are the simplest method of making a silhouette, one that's been around since time began.

In the 18th century, silhouettes were big business. It was a way to capture a likeness before the era of the camera. Using a candle to cast the shadow of a profile onto a paper tacked to the wall, people would document the shape of a loved one's face. Professional artists scaled down these large pieces and turned them into glass paintings, etchings, and other more permanent ways of memorializing the nobility.

Update the concept with an ordinary light fixture, a piece of paper, and a pencil. You'll find that a high wattage bulb will help you; a strongly cast shadow makes your job much easier.

1. Tape or tack a large sheet of paper to a smooth wall.

2. Place a strong light fixture a fairly short distance from the wall.

3. Between the wall and the lamp, place the item or person you want to copy in silhouette. Adjust the position of your subject, the lamp, and the paper until you can see a distinguishable shadow exactly how you want it. The further your subject is from the wall, the larger the cast shadow.

4. When you're happy with the visible shape, lightly

trace around the edge of the paper with your pencil. If your arm or head obscures part of the shadow, just move a bit. Pencil a section at a time.

5. If you like, you can use the silhouette as is, or you can enlarge or reduce it, giving you a wealth of options to use the image for any project large or small.

6. When you're done, you're ready to cut it out.

If this is your first experience with cast shadows, be forewarned; it's much easier to start with inanimate objects or patient adults and older children. Save wiggly small children and pets until you're feeling particularly patient and lightning fast. Alternatively, be sneaky; you can simply trace the essentials while the child or pet sits still, and fill in the details later. Nobody's checking here, and cheating is perfectly permissible!

You'll find the cast shadow method useful for projects like the chalkboard wall organizer (page 74) or the pet bowl place mat (page 82). You'll find variations of this method to fit many circumstances. If you're out with children late on a summer afternoon, bring out the chalk for an adventure that's pure fun for all ages. Position a child alongside a wall and draw an outline in chalk. Repeat until all the kids are shown prancing down the building. Then let them fill in their silhouettes. When you're finished, the whole project will swirl away with a squirt of the hose.

Use Your Digital Camera

Ah, the glories of technology! The digital camera is a lovely cheat when it comes to generating silhouettes.

Many of us are camera maniacs now that we've eliminated the expense and aggravating delays of film. Snap to your heart's content, and then turn your photo into a silhouette that will make your friends think you are oh-so-clever. Here's how.

1. Start with a simple shape. Don't attempt something with intricate minutia. A person's face, your family pet, and common items like a leaf, lamp, or hammer are wonderful choices.

2. While you can use almost any photo, the ideal is one you've taken with your silhouette in mind. Place the subject against a light-colored background. Turn off the flash, as it can cast a strong shadow that makes it hard to distinguish shapes.

3. Import the photos into your computer. Enlarge or reduce the image as desired.

4. Print the photo. Don't use photo paper; print onto the lowest grade, thinnest paper you have. If you want to enlarge the photo to a size bigger than your printer will handle, you can use a copy machine or burn a CD and take the image to a copy shop that has equipment to print it in a larger size. Ask them to use the thinnest, cheapest quality paper possible, because you'll be trashing the printed piece anyway.

5. Cut out the silhouette. If you chose a photo you didn't take specifically for this purpose, you may need to mentally filter out the extraneous images. If you have photo-editing software on your computer, erase the unwanted images from the picture first; but if you don't, trace around the edges of your desired image with a pen or pencil before cutting so you avoid accidentally including or omitting something.

When choosing the paper you'll cut, it's easier to cut through a thin piece of paper than a thick one, though your selection will depend on the end use you have in mind. If you intend to frame a little portrait, select lightweight paper. This method works perfectly for the personalized coat hooks (page 58) and many of the other projects in this book.

It's easy to riff endlessly on this theme. Abandon your digital camera entirely and look through old family photos, scan and print them. This would work wonderfully as an iron-on for the pillow or a photo mat project, or to decorate a frame for an old wedding photo for an anniversary gift.

Keeping It Legal

When you're incorporating images into your silhouettes, here's a word of warning: use your own photos or old family pictures to your heart's content, but never swipe someone else's work to use as your own. Unless specifically intended for use as a pattern, it's illegal to borrow from another person's intellectual property. Stick to your own photos. Your own kids are cuter anyway, aren't they?

Use a Pattern as a Basis

Are you a little unsure of your artistic ability? Are you more comfortable with a set of clear directions and a pattern? Then browse through the patterns at the back of this book. I've included plenty; you can adjust them and play with them to your heart's content.

I've furnished the patterns for most of the projects in the book, so you can make them exactly as shown with confidence. But don't stop there. The chef shown on the wall clock (page 38), for example, would make a wonderfully stylish chalkboard wall organizer (page 74); simply enlarge the same pattern and paint as directed. You can also use the pattern to make an iron-on as you would for the pillows (page 30), but bond them to a dishtowel or curtain instead for a kitchen full of chefs.

When using a pattern, remember you can change it a little or change it a lot. You can tweak it here and there just as you'd adjust the spices in a recipe. Use any pattern for any project. If you see something shown as a frame, but you'd like to turn it into a border for a chair rail, go right ahead. Use tracing paper to copy a section of the pattern with a sharp pencil, and then turn the paper and copy the next section. Repeat as needed.

If you like the patterns for the pillows, for example, but wish they were horizontal instead of vertical, why not place three in a row, making a nice long piece? You can also take the top of this figure and the bottom of that. Break the rules and get away with it—that's my motto!

One easy way to adjust patterns for size is to use your local copy shop. Any copier worth its ink can enlarge or reduce any pattern to fit the project you've got in mind. If you want to enlarge one beyond the scope of the average copy machine, ask the person in charge if they've got a large-format printer. Many do, and though it's a little pricier than the do-it-yourself models, the cost is still quite modest.

Okay, so you've got your design sized and altered as necessary. Now what? The next step is to transfer the pattern to the material you'll be working on. You'll find that transfer or carbon papers are your best friend at this stage.

1. Slip a piece of carbon or transfer paper between the pattern and the material you'll be working on, with the non reproducing side toward the pattern. While it's not strictly necessary, I like to pin, paper clip, tape, or otherwise anchor the layers together so they don't creep. If you skip this step, you risk the layers shifting while you're working, and then you've got a mess.

2. Using a sharp pencil or a ballpoint pen, trace over the outside edge of the pattern lightly but firmly. You can lift a corner of the pattern and carbon or transfer paper to assure yourself that the pattern is transferring well. When finished, lift another corner to check that you haven't missed anything crucial before you separate everything.

3. There's a sneaky little secret that will come in handy if you're on a tight budget or can't find transfer paper. Hold a copy of the pattern paper up to a window during daylight hours, with the pattern side toward the glass. Use the edge of a soft pencil or piece of chalk to scribble on the back of the pattern. Then turn the paper over and you've got a poor man's carbon paper. You'll be able to draw over the lines of the pattern and reproduce it once.

Follow these tips using any pattern in the book, and you'll be equipped to make any of the projects shown and as many others as your time and imagination can handle.

Freehand Your Own Silhouettes

If you consider yourself to be the stalwart creative type—the free thinker who likes to do things her own way—my favorite method may be yours too. You can cut or draw anything you like, no boundaries. Simply pick up your tool of choice and plunge forward.

My favorite luxury is a plain piece of paper and a pair of scissors. Before touching the paper, I visualize every detail of the design so I know exactly what I want to create. Then I snip and snip until a silhouette appears like magic. This isn't easy; it requires time and practice to master, but the joy is in the experience more than the results. Don't require or expect perfection; who needs that, anyway? Allow yourself to revel in the

sheer fun of making something from almost nothing. After all, this is an art form that has no rules.

If you feel more comfortable with a pencil, draw lightly before you paint or cut or stitch your silhouette. And remember, this is art, not brain surgery; if you don't like the results, you can toss it in the trash or cut part of it off and make something entirely new. Since the materials are so very affordable, you can afford to make silhouettes purely for the love of it.

When you're cutting freehand, you need to think through the design carefully before you begin to cut. If you don't, you'll end up with a bunch of disjointed pieces. Even your mistakes, though, can be valuable—you learn what didn't work, which will often make your next attempt better. Art is all about the experience, the journey, and the pleasure, not simply an attempt to achieve results.

When you're ready to start cutting, attack the paper in any fashion that feels right. Start with the outside edge and work inward, or do the exact opposite. Begin with the general outline and progress to the details, or cut the details first and finish with the main lines. There's no "right" way; you can hardly go wrong.

Cutting silhouettes freehand requires experimentation. Don't be discouraged, throw your failures away and forget them. Pick up another piece of paper and cut again. I do that hundreds of times, cutting my way through a vast quantity of phone books, magazines, anything that comes my way. All that practice purely for the joy of it taught me that much of the fun in silhouettes comes not from expecting a masterpiece,

not planning to even save anything, but rather scissoring out shapes to please your eye and your imagination while not worrying about the results.

Use this method for any project in the book. I'll let you in on a little secret: every project in the book started as a freehand design cut with only my imagination and scissors or a knife. You can do it, too, and give your projects your own unique style. If you're not confident in cutting a special piece of fabric or paper, try it first in newspaper or butcher paper to make sure you're happy with the look and feel of the silhouette; then repeat it in the material you have chosen for your project.

This is the method I use because the possibilities are endlessly creative. It's not as easy as the other methods, but that's part of the joy. With this method, you're not limited to something you can photograph or find in a pattern.

Let's Begin!

By now, you're familiar with the methods for making silhouettes. Let's get out those delicious art materials and practice your new skills in the projects that follow.

Drawing Room Pillows

New pillows are often all it takes to liven up a room. Instead of buying fancy pillows, you can get less expensive ones and embellish them yourself without much time or effort. Opt for plenty of contrast to make the pillows pack a punch!

you'll need

A ready-made flat, unstuffed pillow or one you've stitched up

Patterns, page 106

Pencil

Paper

A piece of fabric a bit smaller than your pillow, in a contrasting color or tiny print

Double-sided iron-on bonding adhesive (available in most fabric stores)

Iron and pressing cloth

Pins

Scissors

here's how

Use a copier or computer to adjust the size of your silhouette pattern and print it out, or if you prefer, draw one on a sheet of paper.

Using the pressing cloth and following manufacturer's directions, iron the bonding adhesive sheet to the back of the fabric you'll attach to the pillow.

Pin your pattern to the fabric, with the adhesive layer on the back. Carefully cut it out.

Remove the backing paper from the adhesive and position it on your pillow. Many fabric adhesives are slightly sticky, making it unnecessary to pin, but if the fabric moves around, use a pin or two and remove them as you iron.

Use the pressing cloth again and iron the cut-out fabric to your pillow according to the manufacturer's directions.

Insert the pillow form and zip or stitch it closed.

tips & tricks

It's important to choose a pillow that has not yet been stuffed so you get a firm surface on which to iron. If you can't resist a pillow that is already stuffed, you can use fabric glue instead of iron-on adhesive. Alternatively, you can remove the pillow form or stuffing and re-stitch it when you're done.

Do you have a fabulous pillow that's blemished with a stain or tear? Find or draw a shape that will cover the mess. Then with a few quick snips and a flash of the iron, the problem area is a thing of the past.

Use a scrap of heirloom fabric to stitch a pillow or make the appliquéd silhouette. This worked like a charm for me when my grandma's slightly moth-eaten party dress was too sweet to throw away and not charming enough to hang as is. The underskirt made a silky pillow, and the bodice turned into a fetching portrait of Grandma in that very outfit.

Drawing Room Pillows

variations

You can do the same thing on a ready-made handbag or chair cover (test it first to make sure you can glue or iron on it successfully). This project works well for curtains or fabric-covered buttons too.

A child's portrait (see Family Portrait Coat Hooks, page 58) makes a great diaper bag or backpack.

Use iron-on adhesive to make a quilt for your favorite teacher or grandma, or as a remembrance of a special day. I cut portraits like this freehand at a Bat Mitzvah party. When the guests were at dinner, I ironed them to a ready-made quilt and spread it on a large table along with indelible markers, which the children used to sign their portraits.

Play with scale! Enlarge the silhouette to fit a Roman shade for a visual punch. It can become a focal point if you use strong contrast with few details or a soft accent if you choose colors and textures that are similar.

Candlelight Dinner Party Set

Plain paper and vellum combine with napkins and candlelight to light up your home. These two projects bring a dash of panache to even the simplest plates and stemware. It's not difficult or expensive, yet your family and guests will certainly compliment your efforts. Let them!

you'll need

Pattern, page 103 (optional, but recommended for your first attempt)

Pencil and eraser

Paper

Vellum

Cutting tools

Glue

Napkins

Votive candle in clear glass holder

Candlelight Dinner Party Set

here's how

Transfer the pattern to the back of the paper. Cut it out.

Cut out the liner—a rectangle just a little smaller than the outer edge of the pattern. If you're making the votive holders, make the liners of vellum or another thin paper that allows light to penetrate. If making napkin rings, you can use any backing paper.

Fold both cut paper and liner along the dotted line. Glue them together and let them dry.

Pull the napkins through the napkin rings; place the candle and clear glass holder in the votive holder.

variations

Enlarge the pattern to fit a tall, wide pillar candle. Use heavy card stock so it will hold its shape nicely.

Multiple votive holders lined up along a windowsill, mantle, or shelf look striking. Another idea is to place the lit votives atop shallow dishes of sand outdoors like luminarias to line the path to your doorway.

tips & tricks

Remember the Boy Scout rule: safety first. Never leave a lit candle unattended.

To avoid risk of heat damage to your table, you may want to place your votives on a small trivet, coaster, or plate. Even a nicely trimmed piece of felt will work.

Clockwork Silhouette

Find a ready-made clock you love and dress it up in your own silhouette style. The clock must have an area suitable for embellishment, like the center, dial, border, or case. I drew from my Scandinavian heritage, but you can use any theme to create a clock that suits your sensibilities.

you'll need

A clock of any description, as long as it has room for a paper embellishment

Pattern, page 102

Paper

Transfer paper (optional)

Pencil and eraser

Cutting implements

Iron

Adhesive

Can of clear coat or other protective coating (optional)

here's how

Select a design for your cut-paper embellishment. Remember, you can alter a pattern to suit you or start from scratch with your own rough sketch. Trace the pattern onto the back of the paper or sketch directly onto it lightly. If you plan to cut freehand, just sketch the available space so your design will be properly sized.

Cut out the silhouette.

If the paper is warped or folded, or if it looks tired and shopworn, iron it flat. Freshen it by erasing any stray pencil or finger marks.

Decide where to place the paper on the clock. Try different positions and orientations. If placing the paper around the dial, you might have to remove the crystal and the hands first.

Apply the adhesive and smooth the paper firmly onto the clock. Let it dry.

If you're using a protective coating, spray two or three light applications, allowing it to dry thoroughly between coats.

If you took the clock apart, reassemble it. Hang or place the clock wherever you can show it off, step back, and admire your handiwork.

Clockwork Silhouette

variations

You can tweak the design you've done for your clock to come up with a long slender design. Cut it out and apply as a border on a paper curtain to hang on a window or shelf alongside your clock.

Rather do a mirror? Apply this idea to a hanging or hand mirror instead.

Recycled and Remarkable

I really am the Queen of Cheap. I love the thrill of getting something for almost nothing. Pick up some **ugly** paintings at a garage sale or thrift store, splash on a few layers of spray paint, **add** some bits of beloved-but-odd paper, and you've got a brand new piece of art: a gorge**ous**ly layered canvas.

you'll need

One or more canvases of any size

Old newspaper or drop cloth

Tar gel, acrylic medium, or gesso (optional)

Acrylic paints (any kind of art paint or even house paint)

Brushes

Sandpaper (optional)

Glue (optional)

Pattern, page 105

Paper

Cutting tools

Old sheet music, newspaper, or other decorative papers (optional)

Spray clear coat or urethane finish

Recycled and Remarkable

here's how

Cover the work area with a drop cloth or old newspaper.

For a textured look, use tar gel, acrylic medium, or gesso to create an irregular surface on your canvas. Allow it to dry. Repeat as desired.

Cover the canvas with a coat of paint and let it dry.

I like to weather my canvas by sanding the edges and high spots. I also add streaks or splotches of contrasting colors. If you don't like the look, simply cover with more paint until you're satisfied. Let it dry before continuing.

If you want more layers, pull out leftover art supplies such as gold leaf, metallic acrylic paints, or tissue paper. Use the glue, tar gel, or acrylic medium to attach them as embellishments on your canvas.

Cut out simple silhouettes freehand, as I've done with these pears, or trace a pattern onto your chosen paper and cut it out.

Use more acrylic medium or some glue to adhere the cut paper to the canvas. If you have other papers such as old family letters, sheet music, wallpaper, or newspaper, add them as desired.

Optionally (but recommended), finish with a light spray of clear protective coating.

tips & tricks

For a project like this, it's easy to keep going until the canvas is crowded. Resist that temptation and stop before you reach the cluttered look. Keep a few spaces in your design for the eye to rest.

You can use almost any paper for the canvas: Wallpaper, newspaper, tissue, and plain text-weight papers are all good choices. If the paper is fine or thin, you'll want to test it with the adhesive to make sure the color won't run in an unpleasant way.

If you have a paper that's too precious to wreck, simply photocopy or scan and print it, and then use the copy.

Playful Storage Boxes

When people come into my studio, they often stop just inside the door and say, "It's so imaginative … and clean!" My secret is hiding clutter in boxes and suitcases scrounged from garage sales. By decorating them with silhouettes, I manage to camouflage my storage as "art."

you'll need

Covered boxes, any size or configuration

Spray paint or large sheets of gift-wrapping

Patterns, page 107

Paper

Pencil and eraser

Pattern (optional)

Cutting tools

Iron

Glue or other adhesive

Spray clear coat or other protective covering (optional)

here's how

Buy or scrounge a lidded box of any type. Cover it with spray paint or gift-wrapping.

Pencil sketch or transfer a pattern to the paper you're going to use for the silhouette. Cut out the design.

If your cut paper gets rumpled or creased, or if it's been warped, iron it crisp again.

Apply glue or other adhesive and press the cut paper firmly to the box.

Optionally, spray the box and your design with a protective covering that will help protect it.

Fill the box and stack several together. Depending on how many boxes you need, you could create a whole silhouette landscape.

Playful Storage Boxes

tips & tricks

Use a few scraps to make a tag that identifies the contents of the box. My storage boxes have tags tied with ribbon or glued to the sides. Follow your own heart as far as embellishments or leave them simple for a more classic look. Either way, your supplies will be at your fingertips.

Pocket Window Shade

If you have a view that's less than picturesque, camouflage it! Here's one solution that still allows the light to come in to brighten your day. Best of all, it's personal, it's handmade, and it can change with the seasons.

you'll need

Measuring tape or stick

A piece of thin, gauzy fabric a little
   larger than your window

Needle and colorless plastic thread

Piece of tulle, just smaller than the
   fabric above

Cutting tools

Pins

Paper

Patterns, page 121

Pencil and eraser

Curtain rod

here's how

Measure the window and hem the fabric to fit, making a casing across the top for the rod to slip through.

Determine the size for the tulle pockets that will hold your silhouettes. Allow enough room so the silhouettes neither crowd one another nor look sparse. I prefer pockets that measure around 6 to 8 inches (15 to 20 cm) square.

Cut the tulle into long, thin strips that measure the predetermined height of each pocket. Make your tulle strips just a little shorter than the width of your curtain.

here's how (continued)

Pin the tulle to the back of your curtain. Use more pins to indicate the width of each individual pocket.

Stitch the pockets onto the fabric using long running stitches.

If you're using a pattern, trace it onto the paper. If you prefer, you can easily cut simple shapes freehand or sketch just a hint of an idea and then cut them out.

Run the curtain rod through the casing, tuck the cut paper silhouettes into the pockets, and hang it up.

variations

Why not enlarge on the idea and curtain off a romantic little niche to hide your craft supplies in the corner of the guest room?

You can make a pocket curtain for the kitchen and add an extra little pocket of tulle on the front, just the right size to hold a recipe card.

If you make a pocket curtain using a heavier fabric, stitch the tulle on the front. You can use the pockets to hold your scissors, thread, and other craft supplies, turning a disorganized mess into a charming display. The tulle doesn't show much if you buy a color similar to the background fabric.

tips & tricks

You can change the silhouettes in the pocket window shade to coincide with the seasons or to celebrate a special occasion. Cut birthday candle shapes and letters for a special greeting, or make a spring floral or snowflake curtain. Snip some Christmas trees, Valentine hearts, or anything else that suits your fancy.

Because they are so small, these little paper-cut projects make a wonderful take-along project for those moments you're stuck waiting in the doctor's office or sitting on the sidelines before your child's soccer game begins. Tuck a few sheets of paper in an envelope and a pair of scissors into your jacket pocket, and you've got a lovely diversion planned!

Classic Framed Chandelier

Silhouettes are all about contrast, like the stereotypical palm trees against a sunset or a cowboy at the edge of a bluff. It's usually impossible to throw crystal chandeliers into sharp relief. That's why they make such a delightful visual surprise. You can use this technique for any image.

you'll need

Three invisible frames

Mat board or heavy card stock cut to fit your frame

Cutting tools, like scissors or a craft knife

Large sheet of lightweight paper

Pencil

Pattern, page 114

Sheet of transfer paper (optional)

Large ruler, yardstick, or other straight edge

Glue stick or a very thick acid-free paste

here's how

To get a shiny look without an edge, buy an invisible frame: one made of a sheet of glass and a thin piece of particleboard held together with small metal clips.

Cut the mat board or heavy card stock the same size as the glass for the background.

For the silhouette, find a lightweight sheet that measures at least as tall as the height of your frames and as wide as the total width of all three combined.

If you're using a pattern, enlarge it to fit the total size of your frames combined. Using the transfer paper, copy the pattern to the back of the paper. If you're not using a pattern, sketch a few key lines on the back of the paper to serve as a guide.

Using the scissors or craft knife, cut out the silhouette.

Decide where to cut the silhouette into segments. Lay sheets of background paper together, leaving no space between them. Place the cut paper upside down on the background paper. Move the design around until you like how it looks on the background. Remember, you're looking at the back side of the silhouette, so you'll end up with the reverse of what you see.

Classic Framed Chandelier

here's how (continued)

Use the straight edge and pencil to mark a light line on the design, indicating where you'll cut. Cut the silhouette along those lines, and place the cut paper face up on the background.

Apply the adhesive to the back of the silhouette. You don't need to cover the entire area; tacking it in place will suffice. There may be small bits that you'll need to attach with a dot or two of adhesive. Allow the adhesive to dry.

Take the frames apart and sandwich the artwork between the backing board and the glass.

tips & tricks

Because paper has a warp and weft, you may notice that larger pieces sometimes warp slightly when intricately cut. Bigger, more complex silhouettes can also crease while being handled. A quick swipe to the back of the paper with a fairly cool dry iron will restore the paper to crisp flatness again, which will help you glue it smoothly.

Easy Leafy Napkin Rings

This is just the thing if you're short on time but want to set a beautiful table. These napkin rings are beginner-simple and come together in a jiffy. Let that be our secret, because your guests will think you spent hours.

you'll need

Pattern, page 116

Pencil and eraser

Paper

Cutting tools

Napkins

Paste or glue stick

Easy Leafy Napkin Rings

here's how

If you're using a pattern, trace it onto the back of your paper. You can choose instead to sketch lightly or cut freehand based on the shape of the pattern provided.

Depending on the thickness of your napkins, you may need to adjust the length of the band that separates the leaves.

Wrap the cut paper around your napkin and secure with a tiny dash of thick paste or a swipe of glue from a stick.

tips & tricks

If you have extra time, try gilding the leaves with a bit of gold watercolor or acrylic paint. Another idea is to use a toothpick to flick speckles of bright paint onto the leaves before you assemble them.

Tuck a slender fern or fresh flower behind the napkin.

Glue little streamers of ribbon behind the leaves or embellish with raffia.

You can adapt the pattern for the leaves of the Pocket Window Shade (page 45) to make napkin rings.

For a special engagement or anniversary party, use the technique described for the Family Portrait Coat Hooks (page 58) to cut a silhouette of the happy couple. Place the portraits so that they are looking at one another.

Try this project with different themes—stars and stripes for Independence Day, clown faces for a child's birthday, or roses for a romantic occasion.

Special Occasion Flower Sensation

Fresh flowers deserve a fresh presentation. If you're on a budget, you'll be glad to know that this project is as easy on the wallet as it is on the eyes. Because it's quick to make, you can whip up a new one for each season or occasion.

you'll need

An empty jar or can

Paper

Patterns, pages 106 and 109

Pencil and eraser

Cutting tools

Heavy card stock

Glue

Ribbons, glitter, or other embellishments (optional)

Glue gun with glue stick

Bouquet of flowers

here's how

Cover the jar or can with decorative or plain paper.

Trace a pattern, sketch a design, or decide what you'll cut freehand. Then cut out the silhouette.

Cut a piece of the heavy card stock into a medallion or rectangle shape. Glue the silhouette to it.

Add ribbons, glitter, or any other embellishments to the covered can or jar.

Use the glue gun to attach the silhouette piece to the front of the can.

tips & tricks

Instead of paper, cover your jar or can with something creative. For example, you can use fabric, wallpaper, or even birch bark to advantage.

Make two silhouette pieces and attach one to the front and the other to the back. This makes your centerpiece equally attractive to all the guests at your table.

Special Occasion Flower Sensation

Use a tiny jar or can to make the bouquet holder and attach a ribbon to each side. Tie the ribbon at the top and hang it as a greeting on your front door or deliver it as a May basket.

You can use this idea to make large decorated cones as well. Form a cone from poster board or book board and glue it firmly with the glue gun. Cut the silhouette and glue it to a medallion or rectangle of card stock, as directed above. Embellish and glue the silhouette to the cone. Add a ribbon and you can hang the cone on a door or wall. You can even tuck it into a glass or cup and place it on a table.

Family Portrait Coat Hooks

Let's straighten up around here! These coat hooks add style to your home while showing your entire family—no matter how tall or small—where to hang up their stuff. With this technique, you get perfect portraits every time, even if you're new to this craft.

you'll need

Paper or scraps of wallpaper

Family members (people or pets) to be photographed

Traditional or digital camera and computer

Coat hooks

Cutting tools

Wallpaper paste and a small brush or a can of spray glue and a few sheets of newspaper

here's how

Choose the type of paper you'll use for your project.

Get the chosen photos ready for printing (page 24).

Install the hooks and size the pictures to fit the allotted space. Determine the relative size of each portrait. I adjust the sizes of the people (and pets) so they appear more natural. If your four-year-old's head is the same size as his daddy's, it will look awkward. You don't have to make the proportional differences exact; just estimate.

Print or photocopy the images onto plain paper. Then staple or clip the printed photos to the paper you've chosen. Cut out the paper silhouette.

When cutting the portrait, I often adjust or add details that aren't strictly accurate. For example, eyelashes seldom show in a profile, but I place them there anyway, especially for girls. When cutting out adults, I'll often perform painless plastic surgery, reducing a double chin or the bump on a nose. Think of it this way: you want people to smile and say, "That's me!" not "Oh dear, do I really look that bad?"

Adhere the profiles to the wall, using a thin coat of spray glue or a thin coating of thick wallpaper paste. Do one profile at a time, as you need to get the paper up before the glue dries. Press the paper to the wall and gently but firmly smooth any irregularities. Step back and check for accuracy, adjusting if necessary. Repeat with the rest of the photos.

Family Portrait Coat Hooks

variations

Do you have an extra hook or towel rack for visitors? When guests are coming to stay for a few days, use a photo you've already taken to cut their silhouettes, and then attach them to the wall with repositionable spray adhesive. What a lovely welcome when they find their towels hanging from hooks marked with their own portraits.

Use large wallpaper scraps and cut out life-size shapes. To do this, tack the wallpaper to a wall and trace a child's entire body on the sheet. You may need to piece several sheets together to get a piece that's big enough. Use masking tape on the front side, which you can easily remove after you pencil the shape on the back and cut it out.

To take the above idea step further, cut out full-size child shapes in multiple poses, creating enchanting scenes for a bedroom or foyer. For a local school fundraiser, I once created a whimsical parade of children running up and down the stairs.

tips & tricks

When snapping your photos, use soft natural light without a flash, as strong shadows can make details difficult to distinguish.

Make sure your wall has a flat surface, as bumps and bubbles will ruin the appearance of your carefully cut profiles.

Resist the temptation to use thin paper unless you're sure it won't buckle when you apply the adhesive.

If you are going to leave the portraits up for just a few days, I recommend using repositionable spray adhesive because it rubs off easily. If you plan to make this project a more permanent part of your décor, use wallpaper paste. If you're a renter, use water-soluble wallpaper paste so you can remove the portraits when you move on.

Vineyard Serving Tray

I love connecting silhouette images to an object's function, so it was natural to think of grapes for this wine glass tray. If you're not a wine lover, try the flowing curves of a water theme or the rounded goodness of fruits like apples or cherries.

you'll need

A tray

Paper

Pattern, page 110

Pencil and eraser

Cutting tools

Iron

Glue or paste

Decoupage glue or clear urethane spray (optional)

Glass to fit inside the tray (optional)

Vineyard Serving Tray

here's how

If you're using a pattern, size your design to fit the paper and then trace it. Alternatively, you can pencil sketch lightly on the back of your paper.

Cut out the design. If it has warped or folded, iron it flat.

Adhere the paper to the tray using as little glue or paste as you can, but enough to stick the paper firmly to the tray.

Let the glue dry; then cover the silhouette with a coat of decoupage glue or clear urethane (if desired) or place a piece of glass onto the tray.

variations

Here's an idea I dreamed up in an inspired moment. I found a very cool vintage melamine picnic plate, the kind that is divided into compartments so your foods can't touch one another. A perfect organizer! I thought, and proceeded to cut out tiny buttons, spools of thread, and pins. A few dots of glue and a protective coat of clear urethane and you're in business.

Grab a vintage drawer or even a deep box that you've quickly put together. Bend a pair of odd spoons into handle shapes, drill a hole at each end of the box, and attach the spoons to opposite sides with screws. Voilà—a serving tray. I cut out a large teapot to tuck in the center of mine and covered it with a protective layer of glass.

Garden Window Scrapbook Page

This is silhouette art at its most basic: a well-cut piece of paper against a contrasting background. It's a simple classic begging to be tweaked, embellished, or accessorized. Vary its size and you can make this project your own as a scrapbook page, a frame, a party invitation, a love note … whatever suits your fancy.

you'll need

Photo or artwork

Paper

Pattern, page 111

Pencil and eraser

Cutting tools

Glue or other adhesive of your choice

Dimensional adhesive dots (optional, available in scrapbooking or craft stores)

Embellishments of your choice (optional)

Scrapbook, shadowbox frame, or whatever you wish for an end use

here's how

Measure your artwork or photo and lightly pencil that shape onto the back of the paper.

If you're using a pattern, transfer it to the paper. You can sketch a hint of your design if you prefer to design your own, or simply cut freehand and eliminate this step. Regardless of the method you choose, make sure the silhouette covers the edges of your photo or artwork.

Cut out your silhouette.

Lay the photo or artwork onto the background paper. Now place your silhouette on top. If you need to trim the photo, pencil a very light line along the outer edge of the silhouette to serve as a guide. Cut just inside this line. Double-check to make sure it's perfect. Do you like the placement? If yes, you're ready to trim your photo or artwork.

Apply glue sparingly around the edge of the silhouette where it overlaps the photo or art. Carefully lay the silhouette onto the front of your photo or artwork. You'll want to get it exactly right the first time; moving it around or shifting may leave an ugly mess.

Now you're ready to adhere the photo and silhouette to the background paper. If you want a dimensional look, you can use dimensional self-adhesive dots or pieces of foam board to elevate the piece from the background. If you want a sleek appearance, glue them flat.

Garden Window Scrapbook Page

here's how (continued)

If you want to embellish, add more cut paper, buttons, glitter, vintage paper, gold leaf, seashells, dried floral elements or feathers … whatever suits your fancy. Apply them to the silhouette, the photo or artwork, or the background.

Put your finished piece into a frame or scrapbook, or use it in whatever manner you've chosen.

variations

For an unforgettably special letter, hand write a message on acid free paper and use that instead of a photo or piece of art. Use an envelope large enough to hold your finished piece without folding it, and line the envelope with matching paper if you like.

You can skip the background paper entirely and use your wall instead, making a family photo album that runs down the hallway, with each photo uniquely framed in a silhouette.

tips & tricks

Layering fascinates me, so I love adding borders at varying heights. I also like adding bits of vintage paper that peeks out from beneath the edges of the silhouette.

Embellish your piece with extras reminiscent of the theme. If your photo shows your child's birthday party, weave a ribbon from her present through the background paper. If you're featuring a trip through Europe, include train tickets or a feather found in a park.

To me, this project is like the classic shortcake: great plain or easily transformed into something grand enough to befit royalty. Try variations in color, embellishments, and complexity for a wide variety of looks.

Glass Plate Special

Whether it's for your dining room or your living room, a thoughtfully arranged design—paired with the gloss and gleam of glass—delivers a quiet finishing touch. You'll be amazed at how easy it is to create these future family heirlooms.

you'll need

Clear glass plate

Pattern, page 125

Paper or contact paper

Cutting tools

Vellum adhesive or a laminating machine with an adhesive cartridge (if you're using paper)

Pattern (optional)

Pencil and eraser

Spray paint

Old newspaper

Glass Plate Special

here's how

Snip off a tiny corner of your paper or contact paper, apply any adhesive you're planning to use, and press it onto the back of the plate to be certain you're achieving a gapless, tight bond that's invisible from the front. If you don't like how it looks, try a different material and repeat until you're happy with the appearance (see Tips and Tricks).

If you're using an adhesive that comes in sheet form, apply it now to the back of your paper. If not, skip to the next step.

Sketch the design or transfer the pattern onto the back of your paper or contact paper. Cut it out.

Apply any necessary adhesive or peel off the non-stick backing paper. Adhere the paper to the back of the plate. Let it dry if necessary.

Check to make sure the bond is very tight, with no gaps. Press the paper to the glass to eliminate any stray bubbles, but be especially careful around the edges. If areas aren't bonded to the glass properly, paint will seep between the paper and the glass, resulting in a messy glob. This is an important step.

Time to spray paint. Go outdoors or to a very well-ventilated workshop and spread out newspaper. Don't attempt this indoors or on a windy day; it's an invitation to disaster. Hold the can 6 to 8 inches (15 to 20 cm) away from the plate and use sweeping strokes to give the plate a light coat of spray paint. Let it dry and then repeat this step until the back of the plate is covered thoroughly.

tips & tricks

When you're shopping, look for clear glass plates that are smooth and rather flat. Your design area is restricted to the area that's flat or nearly so. Plates that have a sharp lip on the bottom leave very little space for the cut paper silhouette.

Because many adhesives are visible on glass, you cannot use glues for this project. Special no-show adhesives work better. Look for special vellum adhesive or a laminating machine with an adhesive cartridge. Both are available in the scrapbooking section of craft stores.

Are you on a tight budget but need a gift? This project makes a wonderfully sentimental wedding or anniversary gift. Use the digital photo method (page 24) to make portraits of the couple. Attach them to the bottom of the plate facing one another.

Celebration Ornaments

Festive tree designs are not just for December anymore. These layered paper confections are simple enough that you can easily whip up a big batch to create ornaments for Christmas, Valentine's Day, Independence Day, family birthdays, Easter … any day you want to celebrate.

you'll need

Paper

Patterns, page 112 (optional)

Pencil and eraser

Cutting tools

Glitter and other embellishments of your choice

Dimensional dots (optional, found in craft and scrapbooking stores)

Glue

Ribbon, string, or embroidery floss

Hot glue gun with glue sticks (optional)

here's how

If you're using a pattern, transfer it to the back of the paper. Alternately, sketch an idea of your own. Cut out all the pieces.

Embellish the various pieces with glitter, beads, or whatever you like. I like to treat my ornaments as I do a cupcake: sprinkled liberally with goodies. You can't go over the top with an ornament.

Use dimensional dots or glue to stack the pieces atop one another. Let them dry thoroughly.

Now glue on the ribbon from which your ornament will hang. I use a glue gun because it anchors the ribbon quickly and securely, eliminating the risk that your ribbon will fall off at an inconvenient moment, but you can use whatever you like best.

Celebration Ornaments

variations

Fold a piece of card stock in half and cut a fancy edge. Write a greeting on the bottom and add a couple pieces of double stick tape to the upper portion. Gently press an ornament onto the tape. Send as a greeting card with a removable ornament for your friend to save and enjoy.

Why not make a three-dimensional ornament? After you finish two identical ornaments, use the craft knife to cut halfway down the center on one and halfway up through the center on another. If you make the cut the thickness of the ornament, you can slide the two together and glue them at right angles.

You can create a coordinating garland too. Make several ornaments. Attach them to one long ribbon, leaving about 12 inches (30.5 cm) on each end.

tips & tricks

Here's a two-for-one cheat: If you use a craft knife carefully when you cut, you can use both the inside piece and the outer one, which will give you two usable pieces from each one you cut out.

Ruff Outline

A chalkboard has a retro feel that will delight you and excite your child. Using the cast shadow method, you'll find this project quick and easy, with a powerful graphic appeal. I created a silhouette of my puppy, but you can use any simple shape that fits the décor of your room.

you'll need

- A lamp
- A model
- Large sheet of lightweight paper
- Pencil
- Cutting tools
- Masking tape
- Paintbrushes
- Chalkboard paint
- Chalk
- Ribbon or string

here's how

Follow the instructions for casting a shadow (page 23), tracing around it. Cut out the shape.

Using a few pieces of masking tape, tape the paper silhouette up on the wall. Then trace around the edges lightly with a pencil.

Using a narrow brush and chalkboard paint, follow the outline you've penciled onto the wall. Fill in the silhouette with the larger brush. Let the paint dry, and repeat with another coat or two until you have good coverage and no bare spots showing through.

Rub a piece of chalk over the entire area, and then wipe it off with a damp cloth.

Hang a piece of chalk next to your silhouette wall organizer with a piece of string or ribbon.

Ruff Outline

variations

Vegetable or fruit shapes make for a whimsical kitchen décor and a convenient spot to scrawl the grocery list.

Near a classroom door, a chalkboard for homework reminders can be decorative as well as useful.

Paint silhouette shadows on the sidewalk or driveway for the children to use as canvases for hours of outdoor play. Just give them a piece of chalk.

tips & tricks

Chalkboard paint is easy to find in black or green, but it's easy to mix your own in a color to match your décor. Pour a cup of matte finish latex paint into a bowl. Stir in three tablespoons of tile grout and stir. Use it to paint a chalkboard on any surface.

Flight Desk

Most office décor is b-o-o-r-ring. Wake up your space with an imaginative desk set that reflects your personality or business. Because office accessories often involve oddly shaped pieces, good designs can be a challenge to find. Adjust or crop shapes to fit, or use the patterns provided here.

you'll need

Purchased desk set and organizers

Paper

Pencil and eraser

Patterns, page 113

Cutting tools

Iron

Glue

Protective coating (optional)

Cutting tools

Flight Desk

here's how

Lightly pencil sketch a design or transfer a pattern to the back of the paper and cut it out. If the paper has warped, you may need to iron it so it's crisp and flat.

Apply an even coat of glue or other adhesive to the cut paper and stick it firmly to the desk set. Let it dry completely.

As an optional (but recommended) step, spray it with a protective coating.

variations

Why keep this fun idea in the office? The entryway of a home is often a catchall for mail, school papers, and keys. Stock that messy area with a few well-placed decorated boxes or a stacking organizer and the mess vanishes.

tips & tricks

As long as you're giving the office a visual lift, give yourself permission to go a wee bit wild with your desk accessories. Think of it as you would a bright tie worn with that dark blue pinstripe suit. Choose a vibrant color or a theme that takes you on a virtual vacation.

Travel Log

Because you make it with whatever materials you can scrounge, this journal becomes part of your travel experience: a memory in physical form. Whether you're across the globe or across town, use it to jot down experiences and tuck away mementos.

you'll need

A purchased notebook or sketchbook of any sort

Pattern, page 124

Paper

Pen or pencil

Cutting tools (see Tips and Tricks)

Glue stick or other portable adhesive

Found materials, such as envelopes or bags

here's how

When you've found a plain notebook or sketchbook you like, glue a plain sheet to disguise what is likely a fairly unattractive cover.

Pencil a design that evokes a sense of place on the back of a contrasting sheet. Cut it out.

Glue the silhouette to the cover and let it dry.

Glue envelopes or small bags on the inside of the notebook. You can cut and fold them to make them fit. Let it dry.

Now fill your journal with jottings and souvenirs.

Can't find a notebook? No problem. This is an opportunity for creative flexibility. You can use a catalog or book, even if it has printing all over it. Simply get some plain paper, cut the pieces a bit smaller than the page size of whatever you found. Glue them onto the pages and let them dry (see Variations, page 78). You have a charming, one-of-a-kind journal.

If you only have plain flat paper or paper bags, you still have lots of options. Using the tip of a pair of scissors, make small holes along one side of each page. Now thread dental floss, ribbon, raffia, or even a long piece of fibrous grass through the holes along the sides of the paper, forming a small booklet.

If you don't have scissors or a knife handy, you can make a silhouette by tearing a piece of paper or drawing a form and filling it in with ink.

Pet Plate Mats

Pet lovers, are you tired of that nasty mess around the dog's water bowl or the cat's food dish? Now you can trade scrubbing the floor for a quick swipe of these non-stick mats. Best of all, you can personalize the mats to fit your pet or your kitchen.

you'll need

- Paper
- Pattern (optional)
- Pencil and eraser
- Cutting tools
- Glue
- Clear contact paper or use of a laminating machine

here's how

Lightly sketch your chosen design or trace a pattern onto the back of your paper.

Cut out your design with decorative edge scissors is desired.

Use clear contact paper to seal the mats or take them to an office supply store, where you can have them laminated.

Trim around the edges.

tips & tricks

A high gloss finish on the laminated plastic is important because it makes the mats easy to wipe clean with just a swipe.

If your dog is as sloppy as mine, you may be surprised at how big a mat is necessary to contain the mess. Before I made a mat, I filled her bowl with water when I knew she was thirsty. After she finished drinking, I measured the messy area to determine the size mat I'd need.

If you've got a large laminating machine, you can buy a laminating cartridge and do your own laminating in a jiffy.

Pet Plate Mats

variations

If your house is like mine, it's not only the pet dish area that's prone to messes. Make a mat to slip under your potted plants. Whip up a stack of cute little non-stick mats to pull from the kitchen drawer when you need a spoon rest. And while you're at it, tuck one under the soap dish: Cut out a shape to catch stray drips left behind by the scrubbies and detergents beside the kitchen sink (or even under it).

Are you in a whimsical mood? Cut a doggie portrait from newspaper using pinking shears. Once it's laminated, you'll have a keepsake as well as a useful mat.

You can use digital photo or cast shadow techniques (page 23) to make silhouettes of the faces of your children; then laminate them and use them as placemats. Consider using bright brights, à la Andy Warhol, maybe even using your fancy scissors. They make a great-looking birthday party table, and the mats are fun take-home favors afterward.

A Flock of Storage Jars

Store pasta, rice, or dried beans in jars adorned with chefs and waiters. Keep prized marbles or captured insects in glass jars covered with running boys. Every room in the house looks neater when the clutter is confined within an attractive storage container.

you'll need

Glass containers

Vellum or other lightweight paper or self-adhesive vinyl of your choice

Pattern, page 105

Pencil and eraser

Glue or other adhesive

Cutting tools

Decorative edge scissors and hole punch (optional)

A Flock of Storage Jars

here's how

Trace a pattern or sketch a design onto the paper or self-adhesive vinyl. Make sure the size of the image fits nicely inside the container. Cut out your design.

Use a small scrap of leftover paper and a dab of adhesive as a test to see whether the adhesive shows on the glass. If it does, use as little as possible and place it mostly in an area that's less visible, such as the back of the container.

Place the design inside the glass and smooth it down to create a good bond.

Using scissors and hole punches (if desired), cut a decorative edging to complement your central design.

variations

Use an adaptation of this idea to etch glass. Purchase some etching cream at a craft store. Cut self-adhesive vinyl into the design of your choice and stick it to the outside of the glass item, making sure there are no gaps or bubbles. Apply the etching cream, following the manufacturer's directions. After rinsing, remove the self-adhesive vinyl and use the item as you would any other glassware.

You could apply this technique to your windows as a substitute for curtains or draperies. Etch the inside of the window as described above.

tips & tricks

I have a handy little laminating machine, which I use to attach a sheet of adhesive to a piece of paper. I cut the paper and peel the backing off, leaving me with a silhouette that works just like a sticker. It's very handy for projects like this when typical glue might show in an unsightly manner. You can find these inexpensive machines at well-stocked craft stores.

Floral Foursome Coasters

Dress up blank tiles from a home improvement store, and you'll turn a common bathroom wall fixture into a decorative accessory for a fancy party. With your imagination and a few simple steps, you can indulge your inner hostess.

you'll need

Paper

Pencil and eraser

Pattern, page 117

Cutting tools

Tiles that measure 3–4 inches (7.6–10.2 cm) in diameter

Glue or other adhesive

Spray clear coat or other protective finish

Felt

here's how

Make a little sketch or transfer your chosen pattern to the paper. Cut it out.

Glue the paper to the tile.

Spray the tile with several coats of protective finish, letting it dry between coats.

Cut the felt just a bit smaller than the tile and glue it to the bottom. Let it dry.

Repeat for each tile you want. Make a whole set!

variations

You can purchase transfer sheets and use a copier or laser printer to make decals, which you can then apply to the tile or to other heat-proof products. Then bake the tile in a regular home oven to bond the decal to the item. This gives you a dishwasher-proof product.

Use a large tile, and you can make a trivet to use when you want to put a hot dish on the table.

Larger Than Life Silhouettes

If a little chocolate is good, a lot must be better. The same goes for silhouettes. I sliced giant silhouettes from a foam board I'd covered with bright papers and paints. These big-time pieces can be an eye-popping refresher, and they're so easy you can create them in no time.

you'll need

Two large sheets of foam board

Paint and brushes or spray paint (optional)

Large sheets of very lightweight decorative paper (optional)

Pencil and eraser

Pattern, page 118

Craft knife with sharp blade

Large sheets of medium weight paper

Glue gun and a generous supply of glue sticks

Fishing line or strong string

Old newspaper (optional)

here's how

If you want a colored background, paint or cover the large background piece of foam board with paper.

If you want a contrasting pattern on the background, sketch some swirls or other simple shapes onto a medium weight large sheet of paper and cut them out.

Decide on a large silhouette shape and sketch or transfer it to the back of the foam board. If desired, cover the front of your icon with paper or paint. Let it dry.

Using a sharp new blade, cut the foam board along the lines you've sketched. Don't even attempt to use scissors; foam board is too thick to cut with scissors effectively.

Lay the large silhouette shape on the background foam board. Arrange the background patterns as desired. When satisfied, glue down the patterns and let them dry.

Adhere the cut foam board to the background sheet using the glue gun. Don't skimp on glue; using plenty will give you the strong bond you want.

Use hot glue to attach a loop of fishing line or string to the back of the background board. Hang your artwork on the wall.

Larger Than Life Silhouettes

variations

Try a subject matter that contrasts strongly with the scale of the project. Snails, seedlings, shoes, silverware, needles and thread, garden tools, and so many other small objects look stunning when enlarged and cut from foam board.

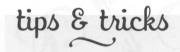

tips & tricks

Well-stocked craft stores carry, in the wood burning section, a tool with special knife blades designed to make slicing through foam board as easy as a hot knife through butter. The addition of a heat element enables you to turn corners far more sharply than you can with a traditional craft knife.

Shelf Improvement

Snip a botanical image for a shelf full of garden books or a teatime theme inspired by Grandma's hand-painted china. Cut a castle with flags flying for the prince or princess in your life. The possibilities are limited only by your imagination.

you'll need

Shelving, along with the tools and hardware
necessary to hang it

Pattern, page 103

Paper

Pencil and eraser

Cutting tools

Iron and ironing board (optional)

Removable masking tape

Wallpaper paste (the powdered type is best)

Bowl

Paintbrush

here's how

Sketch your design or transfer the pattern to the back of your paper, making certain that the design matches the length of the shelf and the height available. Remember that the final result will be opposite of what you draw. Cut out the design.

When cutting large sheets—especially from a roll—you'll often finish with paper that's warped or creased. Don't worry. Simply iron it back to pristine crispness.

Install the shelving to the wall.

Tape the paper cut-out to the wall. Step back to make sure it's straight and where you want it. Take a few minutes to place accessories or books on the shelf. Does the design still show? Is it too much? If you need to snip a bit here or there, this is the time

Shelf Improvement

here's how (continued)

to do it. Double-check before you paste anything. When you're ready, remove the objects from the shelf.

Mix some wallpaper paste in the bowl with enough water to make a thick paste. If your sheet is small enough, paint the paste on the back and hang it in one go. Otherwise, apply the paste to a small area, press to adhere it to the wall, and then repeat until the entire piece is up. Ask someone to help you if necessary. A thin, even coat that covers the entire sheet evenly is the goal. If you need to reposition the paper, do so quickly because some wallpaper pastes dry fast. Unless you are using wallpaper, don't use a damp sponge to smooth the paper down because other paper can tear or smudge easily.

Let it dry.

Add the books and accessories back to your shelf. Perfect! Now step back to admire your handiwork.

tips & tricks

Paper choices for this project range from wallpaper with a subtle pattern to a medium-to-heavy weight large sheet. Avoid lightweight papers; they are not receptive to wallpaper pastes. If in doubt, test a small snippet of paper before you begin.

When you're designing your silhouette, play with positive and negative designs, especially if the wall behind the shelf is already a bold color.

If you're worried about removing the design when it's time to redecorate, you'll be glad to know that all you need to do is thoroughly soak the silhouette with a spray of hot water and then apply a few easy scrapes with a putty knife. That's all it takes. One word of warning: As colored paper may leave a stain, avoid strong colors if this might be an issue for you.

Shell Collection Photo Mat

Your art and photos are special. Don't relegate them to plain mat boards. Tie the subject to the silhouette image and décor, and you've got a winning combination: florals for a garden photo, seashells for the beach house, or something feminine for the sepia picture of your great grandmother.

you'll need

Paper

Pattern, page 120

Pencil and eraser

Frame (optional)

Cutting tools

Iron (optional)

Glue or other adhesive

Mat board (custom cut or standard)

Photo or art to be framed

Shell Collection Photo Mat

here's how

Lightly sketch a design or transfer a pattern to the back of the paper. Leave space around the edges because the frame will obscure the edges of your mat board. To double-check this, lay your finished pencil sketch flat on a table. Turn the frame upside down and lay it on top of the paper. Does the inner edge of the frame obscure part of your design? If so, make adjustments now, before you cut.

Cut out the design. If your silhouette is a little tired looking or creased, touch it up lightly by pressing a cool, dry iron to the back of the cut paper.

Apply a thin coat of glue or other adhesive evenly to the back of the paper. Position it carefully; then lay it on the mat board and press it to bond. Allow it to dry.

Glue the photo or artwork to the back of your mat board. Let it dry.

While the glue is drying, remove the glass from the frame and clean it. Place the matted art into the frame and secure. Hang your masterpiece and step back to admire it. Who said you weren't an artist?

tips & tricks

Many pre-cut mat boards are very thin, limiting the space available for your silhouette. The look can be skinny rather than sumptuous. Though I'm the Queen of Cheap, even I admit it's worth every penny to have a custom-cut mat board. Allowing yourself plenty of room for the silhouette enhances the design so much you won't miss the extra dollar or two invested in the perfect mat. And when you have a mat custom cut, you get to leave the dull-as-dry-toast colors in the ready-made bin and choose something luscious instead!

Cast a Shadow Lampshade

Set the mood with shadows cast by silhouettes tucked inside a lampshade. When the lamp is turned off, the design remains hidden, lurking like a dream. Switch it on and the shapes shine through, changing a simple room to a magical dreamscape with the glow of the silhouettes.

you'll need

Purchased lampshade and lamp

Glue or laminating machine with adhesive cartridge

Paper

Pattern, page 123

Pencil and eraser

Cutting tools

variations

To re-create this project on a smaller scale, try the technique on a night-light or porch light.

here's how

If you have a laminating machine, run the paper through the machine using the adhesive cartridge.

Pencil sketch a design, or, if you prefer, just transfer a design onto the back of the paper. Then cut out the design.

If you're using glue, apply a thin, even coat.

Apply the silhouette to the inside of the lampshade and press firmly to adhere. Let it dry if necessary.

Put the shade on the lamp and turn the light on.

tips & tricks

To create a dark shadow, choose a fairly thick, opaque paper; lightweight paper will cast a more delicate shadow. To preview how the paper will appear, tape a small piece inside the lampshade and flip the switch.

About the Author

Confined to a fishing boat with a pair of restless toddlers and two avid fishermen, artist Sharyn Sowell used her husband's Swiss army knife scissors and the children's lunch bags to cut out Noah's ark and animals. Just trying to amuse the boys, she never suspected she'd fall head over heels into a love affair with silhouettes.

Today, Sharyn's work can be found on greeting cards, mugs, wallpaper, gift bags, and fabric. Her silhouettes begin with a single sheet of paper cut freehand. Her deft scissors hand can reveal a sparrow's wing, violets in a grassy meadow, jazz musicians, or children at play. She then embellishes the cut paper with calligraphy, watercolor, type from her antique press, and digital enhancements.

Her designs have been featured on NBC-TV and the Style Channel, as well as in magazines like *Mary Engelbreit's Home Companion, Better Homes & Gardens,* and *Romantic Homes.* She's an Artist in Residence for *Victoria* magazine. Her images are featured on products from companies like Hallmark, Lenox, CR Gibson, Demdaco, Sunrise Greetings, Costco, Clothworks Textiles, Dritz, and York Wallcovering. She's the author of *Paper Cutting Techniques for Scrapbooks & Cards* (Sterling/Chappelle, 2005). Her work has been seen in galleries and museums worldwide. Critics call her creations "striking" and "imaginative."

Sharyn spends her days in a tiny cottage studio filled with scissors, calligraphy nibs, snips and scraps of paper, printing presses, pots of ink and glue, old family photos, and birds' nests. "My work celebrates the miracles we see each day if we open our lives to simple pleasures," she says. She agrees with Hans Christian Andersen that "real life is the best fairy tale." You can reach her through her website: www.sharynsowell.com.

Acknowledgments

This book is for my sweet little someone, along with the hours and hours of shadow play in the days yet to come. You are a treasure.

Thanks to Janny Stevenson, whose courage and fortitude inspire me beyond words, and to Barbara Pence, my sister and friend. Thanks to my artsy and imaginative friends Barb Tourtillotte, Anne-Marie Heckt, and Anne Olwin for the wonderfully rare combination of encouragement and honesty. Heartfelt thanks to the wonderful licensing partners who bring my images to stores on everything from greeting cards to accessories for the home, holiday decorations, fabric, tableware, journals and much, much more …

Sincere thanks are also due to Terry Taylor, Kathy Holmes, Larry Shea, Mark Bloom, and the rest of the Lark Books team, whose professionalism and kindness made this book a pleasant adventure. And as always, loving thanks to Russell for believing in me through thick and thin.

Index